WHY THANKSGIVING?

The Pilgrims Started
Thanksgiving for the Same
Reason They Came to America
—Because They Loved God

STEVE DEACE

Post Hill
PRESS

A POST HILL PRESS BOOK
ISBN: 978-1-63758-588-7
ISBN (eBook): 978-1-63758-589-4

Why Thanksgiving?:
The Pilgrims Started Thanksgiving for the Same Reason They Came to America—
Because They Loved God
© 2022 by Steve Deace
All Rights Reserved

Interior Design by Yoni Limor

Post Hill Press
New York • Nashville
posthillpress.com

Published in the United States of America
2 3 4 5 6 7 8 9 10

For Amy, the best mother for my children

America is a special place to live. We are lucky to live in a free country where many people around the world wish they could live.

But why is America so special?

America is special because it was the first country to be built based on what its settlers believed was right.

The first settlers were called pilgrims. The pilgrims traveled to "the new world" to escape from people who wanted to cause them trouble just because they wanted to live for God and love Him the way He alone deserves.

The pilgrims were the ones who thought of the first Thanksgiving, because they had so much to be thankful for in their new home!

The pilgrims came to America to escape from the king of England. In their old country, they were ruled by a church and a king who had lost his way.

He had forgotten about the Bible and what it teaches, that God loves us no matter who we are or how we look, and He only wants what is best for us.

Just like your parents, grandparents, teachers, and others help to show you the difference between right and wrong, the Bible is God's way of doing this for us.

Christians believe the Bible tells us that God loves everyone, rich or poor, boy or girl, king or regular person. He cares for everyone the same. He even sent Jesus, who was God Himself, to help people and teach them to put others before themselves. Even though He was king of kings, He was not born in a fancy palace.

His parents, Joseph and Mary, were poor. He came to earth to save everyone, not just the rich and powerful.

Because the king had so much power, he forgot about the good message of the Bible.

He started acting like he was God instead. He wanted the people in England to worship him instead of God.

He forgot that God didn't care about power, and loved everyone the same, no matter if they were rich or poor.

The pilgrims were upset that the king wanted them to worship him instead of God. They tried to tell the king the truth, that he was not a god.

But instead of changing how he acted, he just got meaner and meaner! He started to punish the pilgrims for standing up for their beliefs. He even put some in prison.

So, the pilgrims had to make a difficult choice. If they stayed in England, they would be in danger. But where would they go?

England had an ocean around it, so they would need a boat to escape the king. And that wasn't easy to find!

This boat had to be big enough to hold over 100 people. It had to be strong, because sailing to faraway places was difficult back then. They knew they would face danger on the sea.

They might run into storms, or even pirates! But they knew that they had to leave England, because staying there would be even more dangerous.

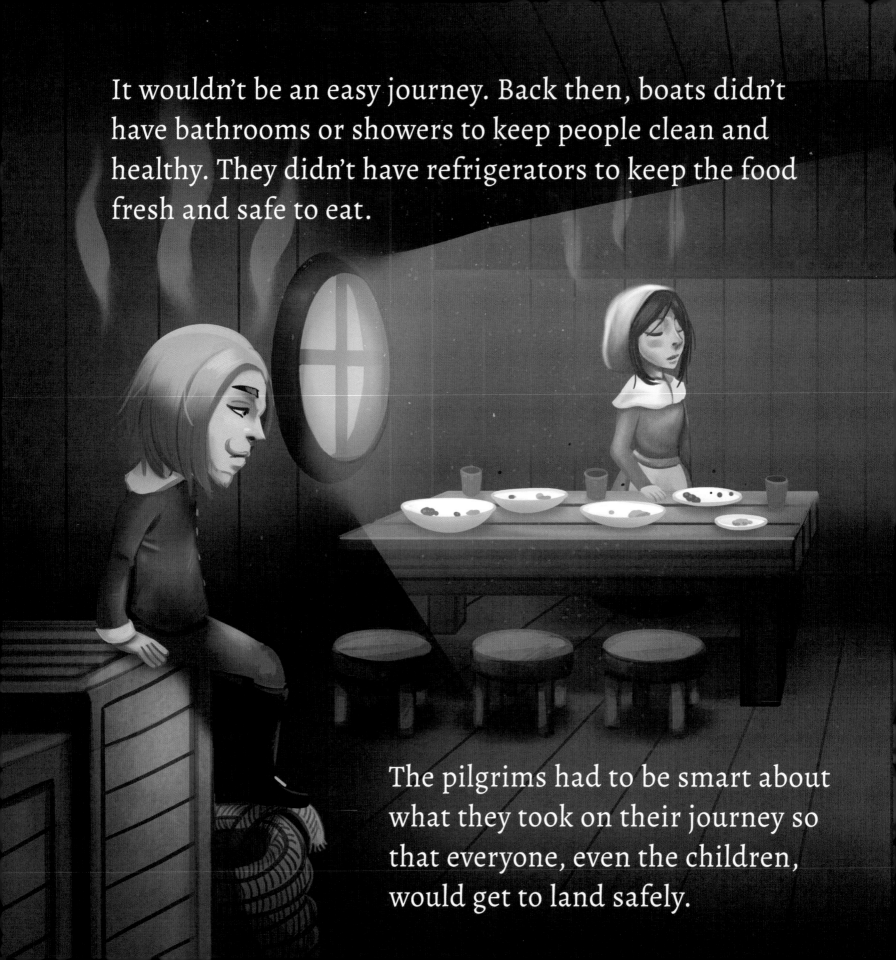

It wouldn't be an easy journey. Back then, boats didn't have bathrooms or showers to keep people clean and healthy. They didn't have refrigerators to keep the food fresh and safe to eat.

The pilgrims had to be smart about what they took on their journey so that everyone, even the children, would get to land safely.

The trip across the sea would take 66 days! There was nowhere to stop along the way either, just water as far as the pilgrims could see.

So many days without fresh food or baths. So many days to worry about storms and shipwrecks.

But the pilgrims had a strong faith in God. They knew God would protect them and guide them to the new world.

On September 6, 1620, over 100 pilgrims boarded the Mayflower, the boat that would be their home for the next two months.

The Mayflower would take them all the way across the ocean to their new home in America.

The Mayflower

On the journey, the pilgrims were very hungry and many of them were sea sick. They didn't see any pirates on their trip, but they did hit a big storm that almost sank the ship!

Luckily, one person had a big iron screw to save the day and keep the boat from sinking. God had protected them on their long trip and kept them safe. Two babies were even born on the way over!

Finally, on November 11, 1620, the pilgrims reached land. First, they landed in Cape Cod, but it was not the best place to settle.

After a few weeks of rest, they got back on the boat and traveled to Plymouth, where they built their first settlement.

But it was a lot of work! The pilgrims still had to live on the boat while they worked on building their new homes. Because it was winter, it was very cold and many people got sick. There was no medicine back then to help them get better.

It took them three months, until spring, to build enough houses for families to finally leave the ship. Now that they had warm shelter, the pilgrims could be safer and healthier.

They did it! They had made their home in the new world, all on their own. But the pilgrims knew they had to write some rules for their new home, so that everyone could live together in peace.

They had traveled across the ocean to protect their faith, so they knew the agreement had to be made for the glory of God. They decided to call it the Mayflower Compact.

They signed it so that everyone would know why they had made their dangerous journey.

This agreement was the beginning of our country. The Mayflower Compact showed that people could live together in peace without a king. They could be free if they realized God was in charge and lived for Him.

These ideas inspired the colonists to write the Constitution and the Declaration of Independence later on in America's history.

Without the pilgrims, and what they believed in, America would never have happened!

The pilgrims spent the next several months building their settlement at Plymouth. Thankfully, they made friends with the local Native American tribe that also lived in the area.

Because the Native Americans had lived there for a while, they knew all of the secrets and tips for growing crops and catching fish. They helped to teach the pilgrims about their new world.

One of the Native Americans, Squanto, knew about Christians because they had helped to free him from slavery in the past. He also knew how to speak the pilgrims' language, which was important for the help they needed.

The pilgrims knew that it must be a blessing from God, to travel across the world and meet someone who knew about their religion and their language.

In the fall, after months of building, planting, and waiting, the pilgrims finally had their first harvest. Thanks to the help of their new friends, it was a very large harvest, with food for everyone, and even more.

They decided to invite Squanto and his Native American friends to this first Thanksgiving, to give thanks for the blessing that God had given them.

According to one of the pilgrims, William Bradford, they even had turkey! Before everyone ate, they prayed to God, thanking Him for His protection and for Squanto, who had saved them from starving when they first arrived.

The pilgrims continued to do well and built up their settlement, always thankful for the blessing from God they had been given.

Squanto was friends with the pilgrims until the day he died, when he asked his friends to pray for him to be sent to the true God in Heaven.

The pilgrims learned a lot on their journey, and they can teach us a lot too! Their trip on the *Mayflower* taught us that God is faithful if we have the courage to do what He asks us to do.

Because they trusted in Him, God provided the pilgrims with safe passage and friends to help them when they were in need.

And that helps us to remember that we can trust God to provide all we need when we live for Him.

The pilgrims also taught us to remember to celebrate God's faithfulness and kindness. To celebrate all the good things God blesses us with, because all good things come from God.

These important lessons that we learn from the pilgrims are what makes America special. We can live in freedom if we live for God and remember His teachings.

God loves to
show us His love.

And He also loves it
when we show God's
love to others, as the
pilgrims did at the
first Thanksgiving.